CONTINENTS

Africa

Leila Merrell Foster

Heinemann
LIBRARY

www.heinemann.co.uk/library
Visit our website to find out more information about Heinemann Library books.

To order:

 Phone ++44 (0)1865 888066

 Send a fax to ++44 (0)1865 314091

Visit the Heinemann Bookshop at www.heinemann.co.uk/library to browse our catalogue and order online.

First published in Great Britain by Heinemann Library, Halley Court, Jordan Hill, Oxford OX2 8EJ, a division of Reed Educational and Professional Publishing Ltd. Heinemann is a registered trademark of Reed Educational and Professional Publishing Ltd.

OXFORD MELBOURNE AUCKLAND JOHANNESBURG BLANTYRE GABORONE IBADAN PORTSMOUTH NH (USA) CHICAGO

Designed by Depke Design
Originated by Dot Gradations
Printed by South China Printing in Hong Kong, China

06 05 04 03 02
10 9 8 7 6 5 4 3 2 1
ISBN 0 431 15796 0

British Library Cataloguing in Publication Data
Foster, Leila Merrell
   Africa. – (Continents)
   1.Africa – Juvenile literature
   I.Title
916

Acknowledgements
The publishers are grateful to the following for permission to reproduce copyright material:
Bruce Coleman, Inc./M.P. Kahl, p. 5; Earth Scenes/Frank Krahmer, p. 7; Tony Stone/Nicholas Parfitt, p.9; Tony Stone/Jeremy Walker, p.11; Bruce Coleman Inc./Brian Miller, p. 13; Animals Animals/Bruce Davidson, p. 14; Bruce Coleman, Inc./Nicholas DeVore III, p. 15; Earth Scenes/Zig Leszczynski, p. 16; Bruce Coleman, Inc./Lee Lyon, p. 17; Corbis/Arthur Thevena, p. 19; Corbis/AFP, p. 20; Bruce Coleman, Inc./Bob Burch, p. 21; Corbis/K.M. Westermann, p. 22; Photo Edit/Paul Conklin, p. 24; Bruce Coleman, Inc/John Shaw., p. 25; Tony Stone/Sylrain Grandadam, p. 26; Bruce Coleman, Inc./Norman Myers, p. 27; Animals Animals/Leen Van der Silk, p. 28.

Cover photo reproduced with permission of Science Photo Library/Tom Van Sant, Geosphere Project/Planetary Visions.

Our thanks to Jane Bingham for her assistance in the preparation of this book.

Every effort has been made to contact copyright holders of any material reproduced in this book. Any omissions will be rectified in subsequent printings if notice is given to the Publisher.

Contents

Some words are shown in bold, **like this**.
You can find out what they mean by looking in the glossary.

 # Where is Africa?

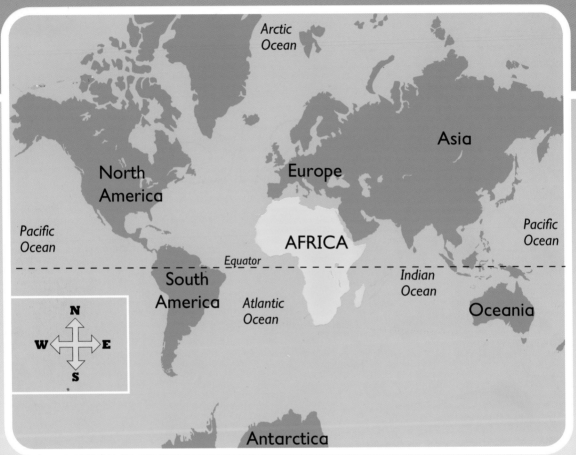

A continent is a vast mass of land that covers part of the Earth's surface. There are seven continents in the world, and Africa is the second largest. Africa is crossed by the **equator**. Apart from the narrow strip of land that joins it to the continent of Asia, Africa is completely surrounded by sea.

Cape Town, on the Cape of Good Hope

Africa lies between two great seas – the Atlantic Ocean to the west and the Indian Ocean to the east. To the north, the Mediterranean Sea separates Africa and southern Europe. At the southern tip of Africa is the Cape of Good Hope. Here, the Atlantic Ocean is very rough and there are often storms.

Weather

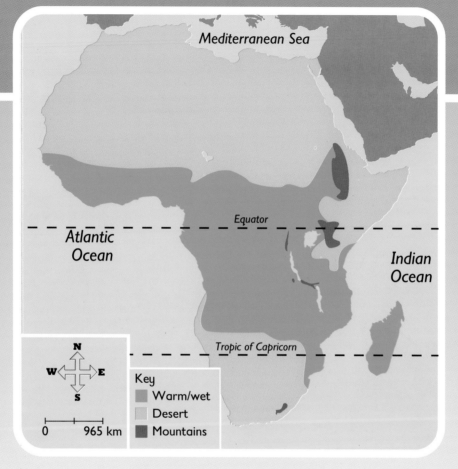

Mediterranean Sea

Atlantic
Ocean

Equator

Indian
Ocean

Tropic of Capricorn

N
W · E
S

Key
Warm/wet
Desert
Mountains

0   965 km

Because Africa sits on the **equator**, it gets very hot. In the area around the equator, there are dense rainforests. The **climate** in these rainforests is **tropical** – hot and rainy all the year round. In the west of the continent there are high mountain **ranges**. The highest peaks are covered with snow and ice.

Namib desert, southern Africa

On either side of the rainforests are large areas of grassland, known as savannah. These grasslands have two **seasons** – one wet and one dry. Further north and south are huge, dry deserts where it is baking hot all year. At the southern tip of Africa, it is warm and rainy in winter and hot and dry in summer.

Mountains and deserts

Mount Kilimanjaro, East Africa

Large parts of southeast Africa are high and flat. Rising from this high, flat land are the dramatic peaks of the Ruwenzori **range** and the Drakensburg mountains. Mount Kilimanjaro is the tallest mountain in Africa. Thousands of years ago, it was an **active volcano**, but now it is **extinct**.

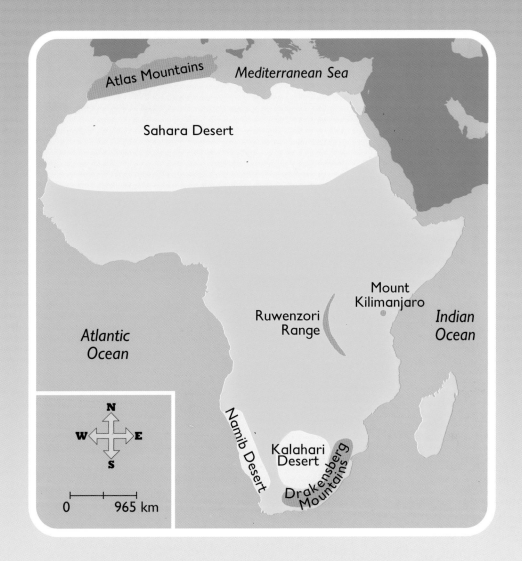

The Sahara Desert is the largest desert in the world. It covers nearly one third of all the land in Africa. In the south, the Kalahari and Namib Deserts stretch for thousands of kilometres. All the African deserts are incredibly hot and dry, with vast expanses of sandy dunes and scorching winds.

Rivers

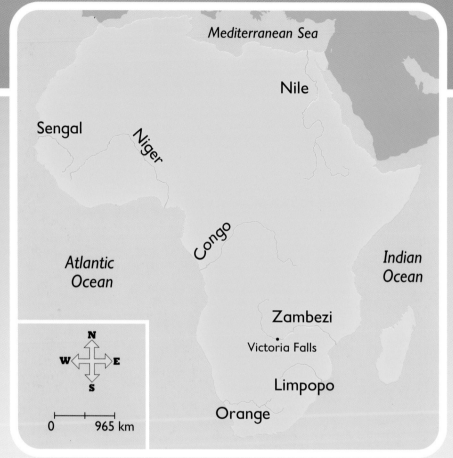

Mediterranean Sea

Nile

Sengal

Niger

Congo

Atlantic
Ocean

Indian
Ocean

Zambezi

• Victoria Falls

N

W   E

S

0   965 km

Limpopo

Orange

Africa has four of the world's greatest rivers, the Nile,
the Congo, the Niger and the Zambesi. The River Nile is
the world's longest river. Two separate rivers, the White
Nile and the Blue Nile join together to form the River
Nile. There are many **dams** along the River Nile. The most
famous is the Aswan High Dam in Egypt.

Victoria Falls, Zimbabwe

The River Zambesi drops for 108 metres into a rocky gorge.
This is Victoria Falls. The roaring water can sometimes be
heard 40 kilometres away. The falls was given its English
name by the explorer David Livingstone, who named it after
Queen Victoria. Its African name, *Mosi-oa-Tunya*, means 'the
smoke that thunders'.

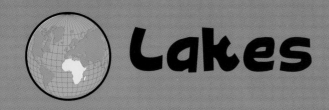

Lakes

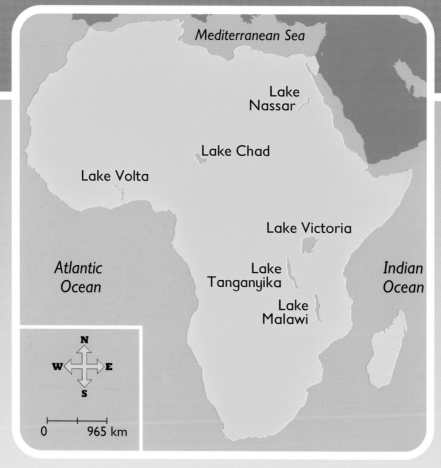

Mediterranean Sea

Lake Nassar

Lake Chad

Lake Volta

Lake Victoria

Atlantic Ocean

Lake Tanganyika

Indian Ocean

Lake Malawi

N
W E
S

0   965 km

Africa has many lakes along its rivers. Some are natural lakes. Others were made when people built **dams** along the rivers. Lakes Tanganyika and Malawi lie in the Great Rift Valley. This wide and deep valley was formed millions of years ago, when land slipped down huge cracks in the Earth's surface.

The banks of Lake Victoria, Uganda

Lake Victoria is one of the world's largest **freshwater** lakes. Many people live along the shores of the lake and fish in its waters. More than 200 types of fish live in Lake Victoria, but now lots of them are dying. The water in the lake has been **polluted** by chemical waste and human **sewage**.

Animals

A herd of elephants in Kenya

Africa's vast grasslands – known as savannahs – are home to an incredible range of animals. Lions, elephants and rhinoceroses all live on the grasslands. Huge herds of zebras, wildebeest and buffalo wander across the plains. Giraffes feed on leaves from the tops of trees, and eagles and vultures hover overhead.

Gorilla, Rwanda

Gorillas and chimpanzees swing through trees in the **rainforests** of central Africa. Crocodiles and hippos wallow in swamps, and flamingos and pelicans hunt for fish in rivers. Many animals in Africa live in **national parks** where people can go to watch them, but the animals are safe from hunters.

Plants

Carvings made from ebony

Thousands of plants and trees grow in the African **rainforests**. Some plants are used to make medicines or food. Some are incredibly beautiful, like the rare orchids found in the depths of the forest. Mahogany and ebony trees are sometimes cut down, so that their strong, hard wood can be made into furniture and carvings.

Papyrus reeds along the River Nile

Papyrus reeds grow along the banks of the River Nile, in Egypt. Thousands of years ago, the Ancient Egyptians used papyrus to make paper. Palm trees grow in many part of Africa. Some palms grow dates and some grow coconuts. Sometimes, people use palm tree leaves to make roofs for their houses.

Languages

There are 53 countries in Africa. Within these countries, people speak many different languages. Altogether, more than 800 different languages are spoken in Africa. In the 19th century, many people from Britain and France came to live in Africa, so some Africans speak English or French.

Arab market in Egypt

In North Africa, most people speak Arabic. Hundreds of years ago, Arabs from the Middle East arrived in North Africa and brought their language and way of life with them. In southern Africa, the main language is Bantu. There are many different varieties of Bantu.

Cities

Lagos, Nigeria

Lagos is a busy port on the Atlantic Ocean. The city is an important trading centre, but it also has many problems. Lagos is a very overcrowded city. Many people in the city are extremely poor and do not have proper homes. They live in **shacks** made from pieces of wood, metal or cardboard.

Cairo, Egypt

Cairo lies on the River Nile in North Africa. It is the **capital** of Egypt and the largest city in Africa. One of the world's oldest universities was set up in Cairo in AD 972. Many tourists come to Cairo to visit its museums. The museums contain amazing treasures found in the tombs of the Ancient Egyptians.

Casablanca, Morocco

Casablanca is one of the busiest ports in Africa. It has many modern buildings and the world's largest **mosque**. The Hassan II Mosque was built in 1989. It stands on a huge platform that juts out into the Atlantic Ocean. The mosque roof can slide open so the courtyard is open to the air.

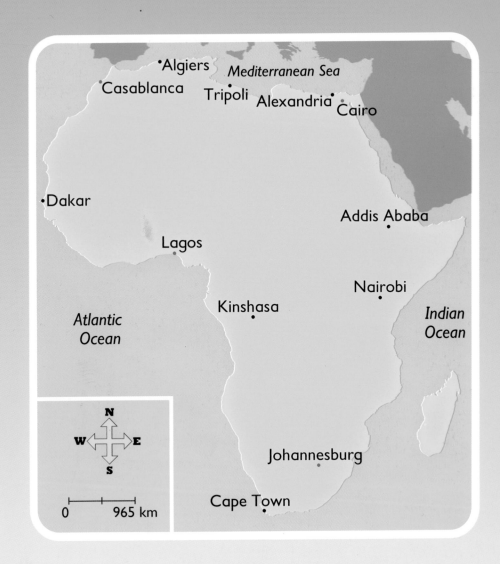

This map shows some of Africa's most important cities.
Johannesburg is the largest city in South Africa. It was
built by Dutch **settlers** in the 1880s after gold was
discovered nearby. Many people came to live in the city,
hoping to make their fortune. Gold is still **mined** today in
the area around Johannesburg.

In the country

Tribe in a village in Guinea

Most people in Africa live in small villages and grow their own food. Everyone in the village belongs to the same **tribe**. Most tribes have farmed the same land for hundreds of years. In warm, wet areas, people grow bananas and yams (a kind of sweet potato). In the drier grasslands, many farmers grow wheat.

Herding cattle in Kenya

Many Africans keep herds of cattle. The cattle produce milk and are also sold for their meat. Cattle herders have to keep on moving to find new food and water for their animals. Herding cattle is a hard life and some young Africans have moved to the cities, to look for jobs in shops or factories.

Famous places

The pyramids at Giza, Egypt

Thousands of years ago, the Ancient Egyptians built a group of stone pyramids close to the River Nile in Egypt. The Egyptians buried their rulers, known as pharaohs, deep inside these pyramids. Close to the pyramids at Giza is a stone statue, called the Sphinx. It has the head of a pharaoh and the body of a lion.

Great Zimbabwe, Zimbabwe

About 1000 years ago, people from all over southeast Africa began to bring gold to Great Zimbabwe. The gold was collected there and sent to ports along the coast. The rulers of Great Zimbabwe became rich and powerful and built a great city out of stone. Only a few walls from the city have survived.

Kruger National Park, South Africa

The Kruger **National Park** is the biggest wildlife park in South Africa. The park was set up in 1898 to protect animals from hunters. Roaming through the park are lions, elephants, rhinos, giraffes and zebras. People can go on **safari** in the park, travelling in a **jeep** with an expert guide.

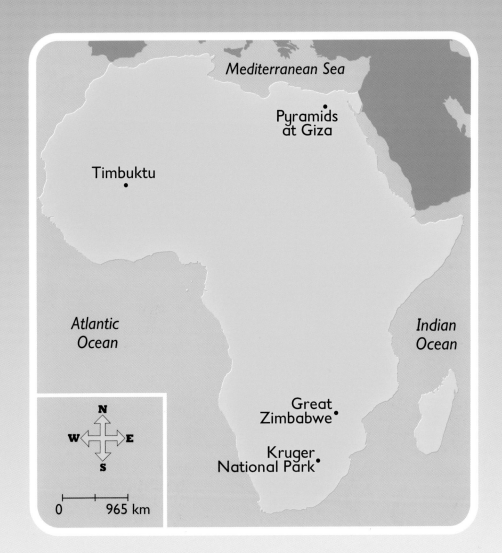

The city of Timbuktu was an ancient trading centre close to the River Niger. It had a large palace, many beautiful **mosques** and a famous university. **Muslims** from all over West Africa came to study in Timbuktu. All the buildings in the city were made of mud.

Fast Facts

1. The Sahara Desert is the largest desert in the world. It is almost as big as the USA.

2. The Nile is the world's longest river. It is 6650 kilometres long.

3. The highest temperature ever recorded in the world was 58°C in the shade. It was recorded in Libya in 1922.

4. Cairo is Africa's largest city. It has over six million people.

5. Lake Victoria is one of the world's largest freshwater lakes. It covers an area as large as Ireland.

6. Africa has more countries than any other continent.

7. The Kruger National Park is the biggest park for wildlife in South Africa. It covers over 20 square kilometres.

8. The island of Madagascar, off the east coast of Africa, has some animals that are not found anywhere else in the world.

9. Mount Kilimanjaro is the highest mountain in Africa. It is 5900 metres high.

Glossary

active volcano hole in the earth from which hot, melted rock is thrown out

capital city where government leaders work

climate kind of weather a place has

dam strong barrier built across a river to hold back water

equator imaginary circle around the exact middle of the Earth

extinct no longer active

freshwater water that is not salty

gorge very deep river valley with steep, rocky sides

herder someone who looks after a group of animals

jeep an open vehicle used for driving over rough country

mine to dig up things from under the Earth's surface

mosque a building used for worship by Muslims

Muslim someone who follows the religion of Islam

national park area of wild land protected by the government

polluted poisoned or damaged by something harmful

rainforest thick forest that has heavy rain all the year round

range a line of connected mountains

safari an expedition to see large wild animals

season time of year

settlers people who come to live in a country

sewage liquid and solid waste from people

shack small, roughly built hut or house

tribe group of people who are related to each other and share the same customs

tropical hot and wet

More books to read

Africa, P. Regan, C. Cremin, Hodder Children's Books, 2000

An Illustrated Atlas of Africa, Keith Lye, Cherrytree Books, 1999

Index